Dedicated To:
The Draniewicz Family
of
Gdansk, Poland

<u>Written By:</u> Abigail Gartland

I was born in Poland in 1905!

Hello, my name is St. Faustina!

I have loved Jesus since I was a little girl.

When I was only seven years old, I knew I wanted to become a sister.

I loved Jesus so much and one night He came to me in a vision.

He showed me how He suffered and died for our sins.

I was very sad about His suffering, and I decided to become a sister as soon as possible.

I packed my things and left my home for the convent.

At the convent, Jesus came to me in visions many times.

In one vision, Jesus told me to paint exactly what I saw.

I drew "The Divine Mercy Jesus!"

Divine Mercy Jesus means that Jesus will forgive and love us no matter what!

Do you want to be more like me?

You can celebrate my feast day with me on October 5th.

I am the patron saint of mercy! That means if you ever need to forgive someone, you can ask for my intercession.

I pray for you every day of your life.

St. Faustina, Pray for us!

Copyright:

Clipart: © PentoolPixie © LimeandKiwiDesigns
Licensed purchased: 1/10/2024

About the Author

Abigail Gartland

I love the saints and I love my faith. The idea for sharing the stories of the saints with little ones came when my dear friends were expecting their first baby. I wanted to create something as unique and special as our friendship. Each book is dedicated to very special people and groups who have enriched my faith in different ways. I am blessed to write these stories and appreciate the unending support of my family and friends. When I am not writing, I am a middle school teacher. I hope you enjoy these stories. I pray for each and every person who opens one of my books to learn more about the saints.

Abbie

www.ingramcontent.com/pod-product-compliance
Lightning Source LLC
LaVergne TN
LVHW061633070526
838199LV00071B/6665